CAPE POETRY PAPERBACKS

DEREK WALCOTT
IN A GREEN NIGHT

Mary's Corner Book Swap
100 Michigan Ave.
Grayling, MI 49738

Derek Walcott

IN A GREEN NIGHT
POEMS 1948–1960

JONATHAN CAPE
THIRTY BEDFORD SQUARE LONDON

FIRST PUBLISHED 1962
REISSUED IN THIS FORMAT 1969
© 1962 BY DEREK WALCOTT

JONATHAN CAPE LTD
30 BEDFORD SQUARE, LONDON WC I

SBN 224 61771 0

Condition of Sale

This book is sold subject to the condition that it shall not, by way of trade or otherwise, be lent, re-sold, hired out, or otherwise circulated without the publisher's prior consent, in any form of binding or cover other than that in which it is published and without a similar condition including this condition being imposed on the subsequent purchaser.

Printed in Great Britain by
Fletcher & Son Ltd, Norwich
and bound by
Richard Clay (The Chaucer Press) Ltd, Bungay, Suffolk

Contents

- 11 Prelude
- 12 As John to Patmos
- 13 Elegy
- 14 A City's Death by Fire
- 15 The Harbour
- 16 To a Painter in England
- 18 A Far Cry from Africa
- 19 Ruins of a Great House
- 21 Nearing La Guaira
- 23 Choc Bay
- 26 Tales of the Islands
- 31 A Country Club Romance
- 33 Return to D'Ennery, Rain
- 35 Pocomania
- 37 Parang
- 38 Two Poems on the Passing of an Empire
- 39 Steersman, My Brother
- 43 A Careful Passion
- 45 Castiliane
- 47 Sabbath, Sacred and Profane
- 48 Orient and Immortal Wheat
- 49 A Lesson for this Sunday

50	Fragments and Epitaphs
52	Bleecker Street, Summer
53	A Letter from Brooklyn
55	A Map of the Antilles
56	Brise Marine
57	Anadyomene
58	Allegre
60	Roots
62	Pays Natal
63	En Mi-Carême
64	A Sea-Chantey
67	Conqueror
69	The Hurricane
70	The Polish Rider
71	The Banyan Tree, Old Year's Night
73	In a Green Night
75	Simply Passing Through
76	Cadaver
77	Islands
78	Bronze

For
ALIX WALCOTT

He hangs in shades the orange bright
Like golden lamps in a green night...
        ANDREW MARVELL—'Bermudas'

ACKNOWLEDGMENTS

Acknowledgments are due to the editors of the following periodicals in which some of these poems first appeared: *Bim, Opus, Caribbean Quarterly,* the *Evergreen Review, Between Worlds, New World Writing,* the *New Statesman and Nation,* the *Tamarack Review* and the *London Magazine.* I should also like to thank Mr Alan Ross for his encouragement and assistance.

D.W.

IN A GREEN NIGHT

PRELUDE

I, with legs crossed along the daylight, watch
The variegated fists of clouds that gather over
The uncouth features of this, my prone island.

Meanwhile the steamers which divide horizons prove
Us lost;
Found only
In tourist booklets, behind ardent binoculars;
Found in the blue reflection of eyes
That have known cities and think us here happy.

Time creeps over the patient who are too long patient,
So I, who have made one choice
Discover that my boyhood has gone over.

And my life, too early of course for the profound cigarette,
The turned doorhandle, the knife turning
In the bowels of the hours, must not be made public
Until I have learnt to suffer
In accurate iambics.

I go, of course, through all the isolated acts,
Make a holiday of situations,
Straighten my tie and fix important jaws,
And note the living images
Of flesh that saunter through the eye.

Until from all I turn to think how
In the middle of the journey through my life
O how I came upon you, my
Reluctant leopard of the slow eyes.

AS JOHN TO PATMOS

As John to Patmos, among the rocks and the blue, live air, hounded
His heart to peace, as here surrounded
By the strewn-silver on waves, the wood's crude hair, the rounded
Breasts of the milky bays, palms, flocks, the green and dead

Leaves, the sun's brass coin on my cheek, where
Canoes brace the sun's strength, as John, in that bleak air,
So am I welcomed richer by these blue scapes, Greek there,
So I shall voyage no more from home; may I speak here.

This island is heaven—away from the dustblown blood of cities;
See the curve of bay, watch the straggling flower, pretty is
The wing'd sound of trees, the sparse-powdered sky, when lit is
The night. For beauty has surrounded
Its black children, and freed them of homeless ditties.

As John to Patmos, in each love-leaping air,
O slave, soldier, worker under red trees sleeping, hear
What I swear now, as John did:
To praise lovelong, the living and the brown dead.

ELEGY
(for Warwick Walcott)

Having measured the years today by the calendar
That marks your seventeenth death, I stayed until
It was the honest hour to remember
How this house has lived with and without you well.
And I do not chide death's hand,
Nor can I hurl death taunts or tantrums
Because the washing faiths my father walked are no more light,
And all the gulls that were tall as his dreams
Are one with his light rotting in this sand.

I shall not hurl death taunts or tantrums,
Nor blast with violent words the yellow grave
Under the crooked tree, where Lazarus lies like history,
For greater than death is death's gift, that can,
Behind the bright dust that was the skeleton,

(Who drank the wine and believed the blessed bread)
Can make us see the forgotten price of man
Shine from the perverse beauty of the dead.

A CITY'S DEATH BY FIRE

After that hot gospeller had levelled all but the churched sky,
I wrote the tale by tallow of a city's death by fire;
Under a candle's eye, that smoked in tears, I
Wanted to tell, in more than wax, of faiths that were snapped like wire.
All day I walked abroad among the rubbled tales,
Shocked at each wall that stood on the street like a liar;
Loud was the bird-rocked sky, and all the clouds were bales
Torn open by looting, and white, in spite of the fire.
By the smoking sea, where Christ walked, I asked why
Should a man wax tears, when his wooden world fails?
In town, leaves were paper, but the hills were a flock of faiths;
To a boy who walked all day, each leaf was a green breath
Rebuilding a love I thought was dead as nails,
Blessing the death and the baptism by fire.

THE HARBOUR

The fishermen rowing homeward in the dusk,
Do not consider the stillness through which they move,
So I, since feelings drown should no more ask
For the safe twilight which your calm hands gave.
And the night, urger of old lies
Winked at by stars that sentry the humped hills,
Should hear no secret faring-forth; time knows
That bitter and sly sea, and love raises walls.
Yet others who now watch my progress outward
On a sea which is crueller than any word
Of love, may see in me the calm my passage makes,
Braving new water in an antique hoax;
And the secure from thinking may climb safe to liners
Hearing small rumours of paddlers drowned near stars.

TO A PAINTER IN ENGLAND
(for Harold Simmons)

Where you rot under the strict, grey industry
Of cities of fog and winter fevers, I
Send this to remind you of personal islands
For which Gauguins sicken, and to explain
How I have grown to learn your passionate
Talent with its wild love of landscape.

It is April and already no doubt for you,
As the journals report, the prologues of spring
Appear behind the rails of city parks,
Or the late springtime must be publishing
Pink apologies along the wet, black branch
To men in overcoats, who will conceal
The lines of songs leaping behind their pipes.

And you may find it difficult to imagine
This April as a season where the tide burns
Black, leaves crack into ashes from the drought,
A dull red burning, like heart's desolation.
The roads are white with dust and the leaves
Of the trees have a nervous, spinsterish quiet.
And walking under the trees today I saw
The canoes that are marked with comic names;
Daylight, St Mary Magdalen, Gay Girl.

They made me think of your chief scenes for painting,
Of days of instruction at the soft villa,
When we watched your serious experience, learning.
So you will understand how I feel lost
To see our gift wasting before the season,
You who defined with an imperious palette
The several postures of this virginal island,
You understand how I am lost to have
Your brush's zeal and not to be explicit.

But the grace we avoid, that gives us vision,
Discloses around corners an architecture whose
Sabbath logic we can take or refuse;
And leaves to the single soul its own decision
After landscapes, palms, cathedrals or the hermit-thrush,
And wins my love now and gives it a silence
That would inform the blind world of its flesh.

A FAR CRY FROM AFRICA

A wind is ruffling the tawny pelt
Of Africa. Kikuyu, quick as flies
Batten upon the bloodstreams of the veldt.
Corpses are scattered through a paradise.
But still the worm, colonel of carrion, cries:
'Waste no compassion on these separate dead'
Statistics justify and scholars seize
The salients of colonial policy.
What is that to the white child hacked in bed?
To savages, expendable as Jews?

Threshed out by beaters, the long rushes break
In a white dust of ibises whose cries
Have wheeled since civilization's dawn
From the parched river or beast-teeming plain;
The violence of beast on beast is read
As natural law, but upright man
Seeks his divinity with inflicting pain.
Delirious as these worried beasts, his wars
Dance to the tightened carcass of a drum,
While he calls courage still, that native dread
Of the white peace contracted by the dead.

Again brutish necessity wipes its hands
Upon the napkin of a dirty cause, again
A waste of our compassion, as with Spain.
The gorilla wrestles with the superman.

I who am poisoned with the blood of both,
Where shall I turn, divided to the vein?
I who have cursed
The drunken officer of British rule, how choose
Between this Africa and the English tongue I love?
Betray them both, or give back what they give?
How can I face such slaughter and be cool?
How can I turn from Africa and live?

RUINS OF A GREAT HOUSE

> though our longest sun sets at right
> declensions and makes but winter
> arches, it cannot be long before we
> lie down in darkness, and have our
> light in ashes...
> BROWNE: *Urn Burial*

Stones only, the *disjecta membra* of this Great House,
Whose moth-like girls are mixed with candledust,
Remain to file the lizard's dragonish claws;
The mouths of those gate cherubs streaked with stain.
Axle and coachwheel silted under the muck
Of cattle droppings.

    Three crows flap for the trees,
And settle, creaking the eucalyptus boughs.
A smell of dead limes quickens in the nose
The leprosy of Empire.

    'Farewell, green fields'
    'Farewell, ye happy groves!'

Marble as Greece, like Faulkner's south in stone,
Deciduous beauty prospered and is gone;
But where the lawn breaks in a rash of trees
A spade below dead leaves will ring the bone
Of some dead animal or human thing
Fallen from evil days, from evil times.

It seems that the original crops were limes
Grown in the silt that clogs the river's skirt;
The imperious rakes are gone, their bright girls gone,
The river flows, obliterating hurt.

I climbed a wall with the grill ironwork
Of exiled craftsmen, protecting that great house
From guilt, perhaps, but not from the worm's rent,
Nor from the padded cavalry of the mouse.
And when a wind shook in the limes I heard
What Kipling heard; the death of a great empire, the abuse
Of ignorance by Bible and by sword.

A green lawn, broken by low walls of stone
Dipped to the rivulet, and pacing, I thought next
Of men like Hawkins, Walter Raleigh, Drake,
Ancestral murderers and poets, more perplexed
In memory now by every ulcerous crime.
The world's green age then was a rotting lime
Whose stench became the charnel galleon's text.
The rot remains with us, the men are gone.
But, as dead ash is lifted in a wind,
That fans the blackening ember of the mind,
My eyes burned from the ashen prose of Donne.

Ablaze with rage, I thought
Some slave is rotting in this manorial lake,
And still the coal of my compassion fought:
That Albion too, was once
A colony like ours, 'Part of the continent, piece of the main'
Nook-shotten, rook o'er blown, deranged
By foaming channels, and the vain expense
Of bitter faction.

    All in compassion ends
So differently from what the heart arranged:
'as well as if a manor of thy friend's...'

NEARING LA GUAIRA

At dead of night, the sailors sprawled on deck.
The wind shakes out its blanket overhead.
All are ribbed equally; all must shipwreck.
The breakers kiss, then bitterly separate;
There is one error flesh cannot repent
Nor motion drown, not while one moon makes white
The tossed sea and her sheets' dishevelment.

Like men in graves, each disappointing west,
They wait in patience for the coming east;
Farewell to that, I have made my separate peace,
Bitter and sleepless as the ocean's curse.

A sailor in an oil-stained vest looks down
To the sea's lace, torn by the raging wind.
'Buenas noches amigo, qué tal?'
'Nada, amigo, nada'
The stars fly from his cigarette in the wind,
A broken man, with a dead wife in mind.
'Mañana estaremos en La Guaira'
I ask him what La Guaira means, he grins,
Says it means nothing.

So the next morning, nothing is green water,
Sun to the left like a starfish, the moon a washed out shell,
And on rust hills, La Guaira, strict as sorrow.
And nothing is a cornet in the plaza, nothing the Morro
Where the garbage drifts, nothing
The bullfight roaring for six thousand tickets,
Nothing Christ's blood forgotten
In the arena of the free cathedral.

Nothing the soldiers drilling in the square,
And the green fountain with its sacrament,
Señor, we have joined a different detachment.

Nothing her mouth, my east and crimson west,
Nothing our restless, separated sleep;
Nothing is bitter and is very deep.

CHOC BAY

Slowly daybreak is blown
Through the conch shell's horn
To the sea, waking with birds;
And slowly that mote
In the heaven's eye climbs, the hawk
Over the falling town,
Then down, dropping down
Over the water with its foam and curds.

Herds
Of driven, bright
Fish in the white
Spray, where the toilers
Hurl their nets from the reef,
Or row by rote
To spread their webbed wishes over
The blue fish flying before some drover,
And the sly shark's teeth.

Grief
In the mute
Mullet's cry, in the soot
Black porpoises plunging the trough,
In the shout
Of spearfishing birds, pelicans, heron-necks,
In gulls building babble over the wrecks;
And look, a diver from the bluff

Splashes the water!
And there, salteyed daughter
Of the sea, that opens its weedhaired tides,
Deaf to the rout
Of waves on the reef-turreted shore,
Deaf to the wailing horn,
She drifts, she rides,
Mary, the sea-lost, Venus, the sea-born.

And I, with a black
Heart, and my back
Healing from history, by the sea
Pink, shell-sharp dawn,
Have heard the story
Of each white goddess whom the waves
Bearing time's bitter legends gave
To those whose lives are circled by the sea.

The blackhanded
Hate-bridled
Fishermen with their haul of sprats,
Have no blue myth to aid them but a prayer,
Venus lives with aristocrats,
It is to the Virgin they give ear,
O mother of Christ, O
Stella Maris, it is
To thee they cast their hopes with care.

Yet not for the day blown
From the horn
Of the conch, pink as her flesh
My mind rides anchor there;
Not for the shell of the wailing dawn,
For Venus dead in green water,
Not for her, windmourned, wave murmuring over
   daughter,
Who nets the mussels in goldwoven hair,

But for the rare
Width of blue air,
For the hawk's heel straying
Over blue fields, I still am praying,
For the wheeling spokes
Of gulls from the crusted wreck,
I kneel to the shell's mass,
With the crab in hiding in salt grass,
And at the bells of leaves I pay respect.

For the morning sky
And the sea, I
Waded in the first, lost light,
My mind as high as the birds,
The salt washing my heel,
For the praying wheel
Of the gulls, and the grey sea's tears,
For the blue and green colours of Mary's gown
Forgiving boyhood that it should have grown.

O herds of the bright
Archery of fish, O Light
Laying your coins on the beach,
I flew like the hawk above time's reach,
I was hero the caves hallooed,
Horizon haloed;
And O dead Venus, under waves riding,
Ark of the Virgin, ever abiding
Mother of fishermen, you showed

It was all a wise
Hoax to my sunblind eyes,
The belled leaves chimed away my days.
O Time, what if I gave the wrong things praise,
The wildest sorrows about?
All that I have and want are words
To fling my griefs about,
And salt enough for these eyes,
For the trapped wheeling of the holy birds,
And my barefooted flight from paradise.

TALES OF THE ISLANDS

CHAPTER I

la rivière dorée...

The marl white road, the Dorée rushing cool
Through gorges of green cedars, like the sound
Of infant voices from the Mission School,
Like leaves like dim seas in the mind; ici, Choiseul.
The stone cathedral echoes like a well,
Or as a sunken sea-cave, carved, in sand.
Touring its Via Dolorosa I tried to keep
That chill flesh from my memory when I found
A Sancta Teresa in her nest of light;
The skirts of fluttered bronze, the uplifted hand,
The cherub, shaft upraised, parting her breast.
Teach our philosophy the strength to reach
Above the navel; black bodies, wet with light,
Rolled in the spray as I strolled up the beach.

CHAPTER II

'Qu'un sang impur...'

Cosimo de Chrétien controlled a boarding house.
His maman managed him. No. 13.
Rue St Louis. It had a court, with rails,
A perroquet, a curio-shop where you
Saw black dolls and an old French barquentine
Anchored in glass. Upstairs, the family sword,
The rusting ikon of a withered race,
Like the first angel's kept its pride of place,
Reminding the bald count to keep his word
Never to bring the lineage to disgrace.
Devouring Time, which blunts the Lion's claws,
Kept Cosimo, count of curios fairly chaste,
For Mama's sake, for hair oil, and for whist;
Peering from balconies for his tragic twist.

CHAPTER III

la belle qui fut...

Miss Rossignol lived in the lazaretto
For Roman Catholic crones; she had white skin,
And underneath it, fine, old-fashioned bones;
She flew like bats to vespers every twilight,
The living Magdalen of Donatello;
And tipsy as a bottle when she stalked
On stilted legs to fetch the morning milk,
In a black shawl harnessed by rusty brooches.
My mother warned us how that flesh knew silk
Coursing a green estate in gilded coaches.
While Miss Rossignol, in the cathedral loft
Sang to her one dead child, a tattered saint
Whose pride had paupered beauty to this witch
Who was so fine once, whose hands were so soft.

CHAPTER IV

'Dance of death'

Outside I said, 'He's a damned epileptic
Your boy, El Greco! Goya, he don't lie.'
Doc laughed: 'Let's join the real epileptics.'
Two of the girls looked good. The Indian said
That rain affects the trade. In the queer light
We all looked green. The beer and all looked green.
One draped an arm around me like a wreath.
The next talked politics. 'Our mother earth'
I said. 'The great republic in whose womb
The dead outvote the quick.' 'Y'all too obscene'
The Indian laughed. 'Y'all college boys ain't worth
The trouble.' We entered the bare room.
In the rain, walking home was worried, but Doc said:
'Don't worry, kid, the wages of sin is birth.'

CHAPTER V
'moeurs anciennes'

The fete took place one morning in the heights
For the approval of some anthropologist.
The priests objected to such savage rites
In a Catholic country; but there was a twist
As one of the fathers was himself a student
Of black customs; it was quite ironic.
They lead sheep to the rivulet with a drum,
Dancing with absolutely natural grace
Remembered from the dark past whence we come.
The whole thing was more like a bloody picnic.
Bottles of white rum and a brawling booth.
They tie the lamb up, then chop off the head,
And ritualists take turns drinking the blood.
Great stuff, old boy; sacrifice, moments of truth.

CHAPTER VI

Poopa, da' was a fête! I mean it had
Free rum free whisky and some fellars beating
Pan from one of them band in Trinidad
And everywhere you turn was people eating
And drinking and don't name me but I think
They catch his wife with two tests up the beach
While he drunk quoting Shelley with 'Each
Generation has its *angst*, but we has none'
And wouldn't let a comma in edgewise.
(Black writer chap, one of them Oxbridge guys.)
And it was round this part once that the heart
Of a young child was torn from it alive
By two practitioners of native art,
But that was long before this jump and jive.

CHAPTER VII

lotus eater...

'Maingot', the fishermen called that pool blocked by
Increasing filth that piled between ocean
And jungle, with a sighing grove
Of dry bamboo, its roots freckled with light
Like feathers fallen from a migratory sky.
Beyond that, the village. Through urine-stunted trees
A mud path wriggled like a snake in flight.
Franklin gripped the bridge-stanchions with a hand
Trembling with fever. Each spring, memories
Of his own country where he could not die
Assaulted him. He watched the malarial light
Shiver the canes. In the tea-coloured pool, tadpoles
Seemed happy in their element. Poor, black souls.
He shook himself. Must breed, drink, rot with motion.

CHAPTER VIII

In the Hotel Miranda, 10, Grass St., who fought
The Falangists en la guerra civil, at the hour
Of bleeding light and beads of crimson dew,
This exile, with the wry face of a Jew
Lets dust powder his pamphlets; crook't
Fingers clutch a journal to his shirt.
The eye is glacial; mountainous, the hook'd
Nose down which an ant, caballo, rides. Besides
As pious fleas explore a seam of dirt
The sunwashed body, past the age of sweat
Sprawls like a hero, curiously inert.
Near him a dish of olives has turned sour.
Above the children's street cries, a girl plays
A marching song not often sung these days.

CHAPTER IX

'le loupgarou'

A curious tale that threaded through the town
Through greying women sewing under eaves,
Was how his greed had brought old Le Brun down,
Greeted by slowly shutting jalousies
When he approached them in white-linen suit,
Pink glasses, cork hat, and tap-tapping cane,
A dying man licensed to sell sick fruit,
Ruined by fiends with whom he'd made a bargain.
It seems one night, these Christian witches said,
He changed himself to an Alsatian hound,
A slavering lycanthrope hot on a scent,
But his own watchman dealt the thing a wound
Which howled and lugged its entrails, trailing wet
With blood back to its doorstep, almost dead.

CHAPTER X

'adieu foulard...'

I watched the island narrowing the fine
Writing of foam around the precipices then
The roads as small and casual as twine
Thrown on its mountains; I watched till the plane
Turned to the final north and turned above
The open channel with the grey sea between
The fishermen's islets until all that I love
Folded in cloud; I watched the shallow green
That broke in places where there would be reef,
The silver glinting on the fuselage, each mile
Dividing us and all fidelity strained
Till space would snap it. Then, after a while
I thought of nothing, nothing, I prayed, would change;
When we set down at Seawell it had rained.

A COUNTRY CLUB ROMANCE

The summer slams the tropic sun
Around all year, and Miss Gautier,
Made, as her many friends had done,
Of tennis, her deuxième-métier.

Her breathless bosom rose
As proud as Dunlop balls;
She smelled of the fresh rose
On which the white dew falls.

Laburnum-bright her hair,
Her eyes were blue as ponds,
Her thighs, so tanned and bare,
Sounder than Government bonds.

She'd drive to the Country Club
For a set, a drink, and a tan;
She smoked, but swore never to stub
Herself out on any young man.

The Club was as carefree as Paris,
Its lawns, Arcadian;
Until at one tournament, Harris
Met her, a black Barbadian.

He worked in the Civil Service,
She had this job at the Bank;
When she praised his forearm swerve, his
Brain went completely blank.

O love has its revenges,
Love whom man has devised;
They married and lay down like Slazengers
Together. She was ostracized.

Yet she bore her husband a fine set
Of doubles, twins. And her thanks
Went up to her God that
Her children would not work in banks.

She took an occasional whisky;
Mr Harris could not understand.
He said, 'Since you so damn frisky,
Answer this backhand!'

Next she took pills for sleeping,
And murmured lost names in the night;
She could not hear him weeping:
'Be Jeez, it serve us right.'

Her fleet life ended anno
domini 1947,
From Barclay's D.C. & O.
Her soul ascends to heaven.

To Anglo Catholic prayers
Heaven will be pervious,
Now may Archdeacon Mayers
Send her a powerful service.

Now every afternoon
When tennis soothes our hates,
Mr Harris and his sons,
Drive past the C.C. gates.

While the almonds yellow the beaches,
And the breezes pleat the lake,
And the blondes pray God to 'teach us
To profit from her mistake.'

RETURN TO D'ENNERY, RAIN

Imprisoned in these wires of rain, I watch
This village stricken with a single street,
Each weathered shack leans on a wooden crutch,
Contented as a cripple in defeat.
Five years ago even poverty seemed sweet,
So azure and indifferent was this air,
So murmurous of oblivion the sea,
That any human action seemed a waste
The place seemed born for being buried there.
                        The surf explodes
In scissor-birds hunting the usual fish,
The rain is muddying unpaved inland roads,
So personal grief melts in the general wish.

The hospital is quiet in the rain.
A naked boy drives pigs into the bush.
The coast shudders with every surge. The beach
Admits a beaten heron. Filth and foam.
There in a belt of emerald light, a sail
Plunges and lifts between the crests of reef,
The hills are smoking in the vaporous light,
The rain seeps slowly to the core of grief.
It could not change its sorrows and be home.

It cannot change, though you become a man
Who would exchange compassion for a drink,
Now you are brought to where manhood began
Its separation from 'the wounds that make you think'.
And as this rain puddles the sand, it sinks
Old sorrows in the gutter of the mind,
Where is that passionate hatred that would help
The black, the despairing, the poor, by speech alone?
The fury shakes like wet leaves in the wind,
The rain beats on a brain hardened to stone.

For there is a time in the tide of the heart, when

Arrived at its anchor of suffering, a grave
Or a bed, despairing in action, we ask
O God, where is our home? For no one will save
The world from itself, though he walk among men.
On such shores where the foam
Murmurs oblivion of action, though they raise
No cry like herons stoned by the rain.

The passionate exiles believe it, but the heart
Is circled by sorrows, by its horror
And bitter devotion to home.
And the romantic nonsense ends at the bowsprit, shearing
But never arriving beyond the reef-shore foam,
Or the rain cuts us off from heaven's hearing.

Why blame the faith you have lost? Heaven remains
Where it is, in the hearts of these people,
In the womb of their church, though the rain's
Shroud is drawn across its steeple.
You are less than they are, for your truth
Consists of a general passion, a personal need,
Like that ribbed wreck, abandoned since your youth,
Washed over by the sour waves of greed.

The white rain draws its net along the coast,
A weak sun streaks the villages and beaches
And roads where laughing labourers come from shelter,
On heights where charcoal burners heap their days.
Yet in you it still seeps, blurring each boast
Your craft has made, obscuring words and features,
Nor have you changed from all of the known ways
To leave the mind's dark cave, the most
Accursed of God's self-pitying creatures.

POCOMANIA
'to a god unknown'

De shepherd shrieves in Egyptian light,
The Abyssinian sweat has poured
From armpits and the graves of sight,
The black sheep of their blacker Lord.

De sisters shout and lift the floods
Of skirts where bark n' balm take root,
De bredren rattle withered gourds
Whose seeds are the forbidden fruit.

Remorse of poverty, love of God
Leap as one fire; prepare the feast,
Limp now is each divining rod,
Forgotten love, the double beast.

Above the banner and the crowd
The Lamb bleeds on the Coptic cross,
De Judah Lion roars to shroud
The sexual fires of Pentecost.

In jubilation of The Host,
The goatskin greets the bamboo fife
Have mercy on these furious lost
Whose life is praising death in life.

Now the blind beast butts on the wall,
Bodily delirium is death,
Now the worm curls upright to crawl
Between the crevices of breath.

Lower the wick, and fold the eye!
Anoint the shrivelled limb with oil!
The waters of the moon are dry,
Derision of the body, toil.

Till Armageddon stains the fields,
And Babylon is yonder green,
Till the dirt-holy roller feels
The obscene breeding the unseen.

Till those black forms be angels white,
And Zion fills each eye.
High overhead the crow of night
Patrols eternity.

PARANG

...the second cuatroman sings.

Man, I suck me tooth when I hear
How dem croptime fiddlers lie,
And de wailing, kiss-me-arse flutes
That bring water to me eye!
O, when I t'ink how from young
I wasted time at de fêtes,
I could bawl in a red-eyed rage
For desire turned to regret,
Not knowing the truth that I sang
At parang and la comette.
Boy, every damned tune them tune
Of love that will last forever
Is the wax and the wane of the moon
Since Adam catch body-fever.

I old, so the young crop won't
Have these claws to reap their waist,
But I know 'do more' from 'don't'
Since the grave cry out 'Make haste!'
This banjo world have one string
And all man does dance to that tune:
That love is a place in the bush
With music grieving from far,
As you look past her shoulder and see
Like her one tear afterwards
The falling of a fixed star.
Young men does bring love to disgrace
With remorseful, regretful words,
When flesh upon flesh was the tune
Since the first cloud raise up to disclose
The breast of the naked moon.

TWO POEMS ON THE PASSING OF AN EMPIRE

I

A heron flies across the morning marsh and brakes
its teetering wings to decorate a stump
                            (thank God
that from this act the landscape is complete
and time and motion at a period
as such an emblem led Rome's trampling feet,
pursued by late proconsuls bearing law)
And underline this quiet with a caw.

II

In the small coffin of his house, the pensioner,
A veteran of the African campaign,
Bends, as if threading an eternal needle;
One-eyed as any grave, his skull, cropped wool,
Or lifts his desert squint to hear
The children singing, Rule, Britannia, Rule,
As if they needed practice to play dead.
Boys will still pour their blood out for a sieve
Despite his balsam eye and doddering jaw;
And if one eye should weep, would they believe
In such a poor flag as an empty sleeve?

STEERSMAN, MY BROTHER

(In memoriam: Julian John)
ad luminis oras: VIRGIL

I

We 'write on water' if our souls are drowned
Within the origin of all life, the sea.
Yet Queequeg's coffin rose and Ishmael found
Those prows a compass to eternity.
And several, rooted visionaries think
If flesh is mortal, love is infinite;
That though our proudly ribbed endeavours sink
In dirt, or swirling sea,
Our souls, like plants, yearn for the shores of light.

But now such simple sermons are like sand
Dispersed in wind, like lanterns crackled out,
Since he lies buried in a strange land.

Not for his bones, anchored in dirt, I write
This elegy, nor for his spirit given
As he believed up to the fishing Christ,
Those shoals of martyrs in the nets of heaven;
But where a wailing autumn strips the year
And drives the rootless, ageing leaves for miles,
I weep for hearts like mine, continually driven
As these lost leaves across earth's barren ground.
Those whom yearspring, dayspring and heartbreak rain
Cannot renew, whose noon is a white night,
Those twilight intellects on the edge of light.

II

Let me believe that Galilee of light
On which he found his calling shall be trod
By the pierced, halcyon feet; that every cell

Of salt blood and salt sea shall mix, and mixing move
In exultation to the shore of God.

Motion is all our truth, a whirling sphere
Of change, decay and ebb, the augurs
Or halcyons of the turning year,
The Crab and fishes draw the dozen zones;
Yearly the cyclic hope renews its round,
The things of sand and water creep and fly,
And draw the axle of the groaning year,
Yet in this ash of energy, the foam,
Where is the soul of my lost helmsman found?
Where, in such waste, must man find his long home?

The sea pursues its cycle as we live,
Indifferent to what trust controls the wheel,
Our lives are mapless, until grief makes us feel
A need to simplify and to forgive;
And then we think of those minds which became
As pure as fire fed the trash of thought,
An imitation of the very flame
By which they studied human change and wrought
A marble quiet in the midst of change,
And had he lived, he would be part of them.

III

I had such faith as yours, but the tides
Of bitterness broke over me, and the raft
Of my saved cargoes perished. Now, what rides
The violent waters of my life, is a mere craft
Of words, and thirst
For those fresh springs of grace, which, as I write,
Mourning my faith's death in your death, derides
That earlier, steady trust
That there are harbours, there are fields of light,
But vision cannot see them for time's dust.

For what has sown us on this whirling star,
And to what end, surpasses human thought,
How He, who makes his gospels death and war,
Has equally the silent raindrop wrought,
That He whose pierced feet stilled the whistling seas,
Bore mercy in the semblance of a dove,
And tore the wound in Adam's humming side,
Could make the immortal thirst that finds no peace,
And then devise a simple truth like love.

Pray for me, father, in the narrow straits
Between the rocks of heaven and this world,
Or if the soul sails on that brimless flood
Down that infinite cavern where the stars
Seem like known angels with their quiet torches,
Unlike this twilight world of fear and good,
Or if perhaps you look now from the porches
Of unimaginable heaven, bless
What gives some hope to the worst human cause,
The final coal of human tenderness.

IV

Restore, if even by your death, my faith,
As He, whose images we are made, restored
By His thorn crown, this life's unwithering wreath
That all shall wear; whose, 'not peace but a sword'
Wearies my struggle as my reason seeks
A mastery of argument with God.

Usurp that monarchy, O temporal death,
Fallen, fallen, greater than my friend
Have fallen; Your hosts of reason gleam,
Disperse like stars that drift across the sands
And bitter pastures of the sea. Descend,
O Dove, enter the open ark I make my hands.

How treacherously do all those armoured bands
Revolt against all reason, like those autumn sheaves
Scythed in the moonlight and forever fallen,
They are the harvest of His coming peace. Their greaves
And pages whirl at the world's end,
They fight their own thoughts in descending night.
Vain energies, with life so long to spend,
While simple plants turn to the shores of light.

A CAREFUL PASSION

> Hosanna, I build me house, Lawd,
> De rain come wash it 'way.
> JAMAICAN SONG

The Cruise Inn, at the city's edge,
Extends a breezy prospect of the sea
From tables fixed like islands near a hedge
Of foam-white flowers, and to deaden thought,
Marimba medleys from a local band,
To whose gay pace my love now drummed a hand.
I watched an old Greek freighter quitting port.

You hardly smell the salt breeze in this country
Except you come down to the harbour's edge.
Not like the smaller islands to the south.
There the green wave spreads on the printless beach.
I think of wet hair and a grape red mouth.
The hand which wears her husband's ring, lies
On the table idly, a brown leaf on the sand.
The other brushes off two coupling flies.
'Sometimes I wonder if you've lost your speech.'
Above our heads, the rusty cries
Of gulls revolving in the wind.
Wave after wave of memory silts the mind.

The gulls seem happy in their element.
We are lapped gently in the sentiment
Of a small table by the harbour's edge.
Hearts learn to die well that have died before.
My sun-puffed carcass, its eyes full of sand,
Rolls, spun by breakers on a southern shore.
'This way is best, before we both get hurt.'
Look how I turn there, featureless, inert.
That weary phrase moves me to stroke her hand
While winds play with the corners of her skirt.

Better to lie, to swear some decent pledge,
To resurrect the buried heart again;
To twirl a glass and smile, as in pain,
At a small table by the water's edge.
'Yes, this is best, things might have grown much worse...'

And that is all the truth, it could be worse;
All is exhilaration on the eve,
Especially, when the self-seeking heart
So desperate for some mirror to believe
Finds in strange eyes the old original curse.
So cha cha cha, begin the long goodbyes,
Leave the half-tasted sorrows of each pledge,
As the salt wind brings brightness to her eyes,
At a small table by the water's edge.

I walk with her into the brightening street;
Stores rattling shut, as brief dusk fills the city.
Only the gulls, hunting the water's edge
Wheel like our lives, seeking something worth pity.

CASTILIANE

I

The GOLONDRINA is a sour hotel,
Redeemed, like Creole architecture,
By its ornate, wrought-iron balcony;
A floral asterisk to grace a lecture
On 'Spanish Art In The Last Century'.
And though its rusty quaintness is no cure
Against the encroaching odours of the port,
Its failing apertures inhale the sea;
Besides, a wraith haunts there whom I know well,
Having created her in noon's despair.

Frail Donna of another century,
A grace of muslin, vineleaf and guitars,
She comes at noon, guarded by black duennas
To flute and bandol music from the bars,
Above the flies, molasses, donkey carts,
Above the clash of voices from the pier
Of stevedores gambling over tepid beer,
And stands as mute as old embroidery
On an old fashioned cushion of the heart.

II

Why should she hide against the dirty lace
Which stirs so still, its drift is scarcely seen
From the hot street? Why is that haunted face,
Dim as an antique faun's, fin de siècle style,
Imprisoned in the grillwork's leafless green
Who can evoke Alhambras with a smile?

Assailed by memory, desire stirs;
Yet that white hand against a rose cheek sleeping
That to the idler makes a subtle sign
Becomes a pigeon from a dark coign sweeping

As the coarse odour from the street defers
Anticipation of dark cellared wine.

Albums of lost Alhambras, swaying cypresses,
Brooding, daggered Moors and fanfares from da Falla,
A sable papa munching his moustache,
The scented note, the fearful assignation:
'I must, I must go now...', sighing, she sweeps
Her jewelled laces up as bells
Shatter the crystal park. The dark
Duennas weep,
They know the true necessity of that sleep
That withers centuries or the virgin rose.
Jesu Maria, what nonsense... I suppose...

III

I stir to smell the male, malodorous sea.
Another trance of mine is moving water.
How would it end? A merchant claims the daughter,
A man who hawks and profits in this heat,
Jeering at poets with a goldtoothed curse.
Girl, you were wise, whoever lived by verse?
The future is in cheap enamel wares.

Yet, Doña Maria, like a worn-out song
That keeps a phrase of wisdom in our ears,
Like the sad gaiety of a drunk guitar,
Like the bright gardens which blind vendors sell,
I watch your ancient, simple spirit where
Its letters flake across the balcony
From the façade of a third-rate hotel.

SABBATH, SACRED AND PROFANE

Heaven's morning breaks, and all our joys are set
From custom, yes; but with conflicting rites
Of lilies in brazen bowls, His Easter sign,
And bell-mouthed glasses with His wound in wine;
Ritual of His passion I may not forget,
Not while through suburbs roars the word; 'Rejoice
In resurrection on the wireless,'
Drowning the swallow's hedonistic voice.

She in the ravaged wood, whose limbs are wet
With dew, calls and recalls when Sunday at the blinds
Woke the barred shadows of your nakedness.

ORIENT AND IMMORTAL WHEAT

> The corn was orient and immortal wheat,
> which never should be reaped, nor was
> ever sown. I thought it had stood from
> everlasting to everlasting.
> TRAHERNE: *Centuries of Meditations*

Nature seemed monstrous to his thirteen years.
Prone to malaria, sweating inherent sin,
Absolved in limacol and evening prayers,
The prodigy, dusk rougeing his peaked face
Studied the swallows stitch the opposing eaves
In repetitions of the fall from grace.
And as a gilding silence flushed the leaves,
Hills, roofs and yards with his own temperature,
He wept again, though why, he was unsure,
At dazzling visions of reflected tin.
So heaven is revealed to fevered eyes,
So is sin born, and innocence made wise,
By intimations of hot galvanize.

This was the fever called original sin,
Such anthropomorphic love illumines hell,
A charge brought to his Heavenly Father's face
That wept for bat-voiced orphans in the streets
And cripples limping homeward in weak light,
When the lamplighter, his head swung by its hair
Meant the dread footfall lumping up the stair:
Maman with soup, perhaps; or it could well
Be Chaos, genderer of this earth, called Night.

A LESSON FOR THIS SUNDAY

The growing idleness of summer grass
With its frail kites of furious butterflies
Requests the lemonade of simple praise
In scansion gentler than my hammock swings
And rituals no more upsetting than a
Black maid shaking linen as she sings
The plain notes of some protestant hosanna
Since I lie idling from the thought in things,

Or so they should. Until I hear the cries
Of two small children hunting yellow wings,
Who break my sabbath with the thought of sin.
Brother and sister, with a common pin,
Frowning like serious lepidopterists.
The little surgeon pierces the thin eyes.
Crouched on plump haunches, as a mantis prays
She shrieks to eviscerate its abdomen.
The lesson is the same. The maid removes
Both prodigies from their interest in science.
The girl, in lemon frock, begins to scream
As the maimed, teetering thing attempts its flight.
She is herself a thing of summery light,
Frail as a flower in this blue August air,
Not marked for some late grief that cannot speak.

The mind swings inward on itself in fear
Swayed towards nausea from each normal sign.
Heredity of cruelty everywhere,
And everywhere the frocks of summer torn,
The long look back to see where choice is born,
As summer grass sways to the scythe's design.

FRAGMENTS AND EPITAPHS

GREENWICH VILLAGE, WINTER

A book is a life, and this
White paper death,
I roll it on the drum and write,
Rum-courage on my breath.
The truth is no less hard
Than it was years ago,
Than what Catullus, Villon heard,
Each word,
Black footprints in the frightening snow.

TIME'S SURPRISE

Fierce dew filled my boyish eyes
For breaking heart, or broken plant,
This is Time's surprise:
Below the pools of pity lies
The heart of adamant.

A STATUE, OVERLOOKING CENTRAL PARK

Turned with the lyre on a tilted hip,
Almost like earth-mothers hip-carry kids,
The Muse hath a stone breast in America.
I rest dark hands thereon, and pray for piece.

ALBA

Dawn breaking as I woke,
With the white sweat of the dew
On the green, new grass.
I walked in the cold, quiet as
If it were the world beginning;
Peeling and eating a chilled tangerine.
I may have many sorrows,
Dawn is not one of them.

NOCTURNE

A tired lady, her frail hand on the banisters,
She climbs to her usual throne in the heavens,
In her white hair, a coronet of devalued stars,
To her box in the ridiculous opera.

TROILUS AND CRESSIDA

Came 'calm of mind, all passion spent'
To Troilus, breaking in his tent;
No thought but the worm's joy in his head:
'The hobby-horse rides Diomed.'

MARRIAGE

Jealous of soul, body fulfils its curse.
The virgin lamp is lowered to its wick,
Too faint to cast the nimbus of God's face.
'Do not divide divine from bodily love,'
Sing the mad fires dancing in my head,
The last is wisdom rotting, while the first
Casts Hell's own shadows round the marriage-bed.

BLEECKER STREET, SUMMER

Summer for prose and lemons, for nakedness and languor,
for the eternal idleness of the imagined return,
for rare flutes and bare feet, and the August bedroom
of tangled sheets and the sunday salt, ah violin !

When I press summer dusks together, it is
a month of street accordions and sprinklers
laying the dust, small shadows running from me.

It is music opening and closing, mia Italia, on Bleecker,
ciao, Antonio, and the water-cries of children
tearing the rose coloured sky in streams of paper,
it is dusk in the nostrils and the smell of water
down littered streets that lead you to no water,
and gathering islands and lemons in the mind.

There is the Hudson, like the sea aflame.
I would undress you in the summer heat,
and laugh and dry your damp flesh if you came.

A LETTER FROM BROOKLYN

An old lady writes me in a spidery style,
Each character trembling, and I see a veined hand
Pellucid as paper, travelling on a skein
Of such frail thoughts its thread is often broken;
Or else the filament from which a phrase is hung
Dims to my sense, but caught, it shines like steel,
As touch a line, and the whole web will feel.
She describes my father, yet I forget her face
More easily than my father's yearly dying;
Of her I remember small, buttoned boots and the place
She kept in our wooden church on those Sundays
Whenever her strength allowed;
Grey haired, thin voiced, perpetually bowed.

'I am Mable Rawlins,' she writes, 'and know both your parents;'
He is dead, Miss Rawlins, but God bless your tense:
'Your father was a dutiful, honest,
Faithful and useful person.'
For such plain praise what fame is recompense?
'A horn-painter, he painted delicately on horn,
He used to sit around the table and paint pictures.'
The peace of God needs nothing to adorn
It, nor glory nor ambition.
'He is twenty-eight years buried,' she writes, 'he was called home,
And is, I am sure, doing greater work.'

The strength of one frail hand in a dim room
Somewhere in Brooklyn, patient and assured,
Restores my sacred duty to the Word.
'Home, home,' she can write, with such short time to live,
Alone as she spins the blessings of her years;
Not withered of beauty if she can bring such tears,
Nor withdrawn from the world that breaks its lovers so;
Heaven is to her the place where painters go,
All who bring beauty on frail shell or horn,

There was all made, thence their lux-mundi drawn,
Drawn, drawn, till the thread is resilient steel,
Lost though it seems in darkening periods,
And there they return to do work that is God's.

So this old lady writes, and again I believe,
I believe it all, and for no man's death I grieve.

A MAP OF THE ANTILLES

On maps to Federalists the Antilles may seem
A single chain, in the bright geography
Of shoals and bays like emeralds in a book
For children; to scholars, they are seas
Of simple tongues and customs, in the dream
Of ageing transients, the Hesperides.
Nothing which I assert can prove them fools
Since men invent those truths which they discover;
Mariner or minister, I am none of these,
My compass keeps avoiding all the facts
To find that South is its magnetic mover;
By force of separation it directs
All active interest towards your shores, moreover,
As a true governor it approves its acts.
Against the slightest opposition, it
Compels all current motions back to you,
And by such licence damns a federation
Which can condone my extradition; it
Is not one country that keeps me from you,
Nor are seas magical that sing of separation.
Are these the Hesperides of which we read
That set a raging strait between each bed?
And so an emerald sea, wild as this one
Seemed to Odysseus a destructive ocean,
Even as he lingered in Circean seas;
Since in no magic port was there such peace
As where his love remained. This is a brief
Ignored by our first parliaments, to chart
The dangerous currents of dividing grief
That make our union a mockery of the heart.

BRISE MARINE

K with quick laughter, honey skin and hair
and always money. In what beach shade, what year
Has she so scented with her gentleness
I cannot watch bright water but think of her
and that fine morning when she sang o rare
Ben's lyric of 'the bag o' the bee'
and 'the nard in the fire'
                                    'nard in the fire'
against the salty music of the sea
the fresh breeze tangling each honey tress.
                                and what year was the fire?
Girls' faces dim with time, Andreuille all gold…
Sunday. The grass peeps through the breaking pier.
Tables in the trees, like entering Renoir.
Maintenant je n'ai plus ni fortune, ni pouvoir…
But when the light was setting through thin hair,
Holding whose hand by what trees, what old wall.

Two honest women, Christ, where are they gone?
Out of that wonder, what do I most recall?
The darkness closing round a fisherman's oar.
The sound of water gnawing at bright stone.

ANADYOMENE

The shoulders of a shining nereid
Glide in warm shallows, nearing the white sand;
Thighs tangled in the golden weed,
Did fin flash there, or woman's hand?
Weed dissolves to burnished hair,
Foam now, where was milk-white breast,
Did thigh or dolphin cleave the air?
Half-woman and half-fish, or best
Both fish and woman, let them keep
Their, elusive mystery.
Hurt, the wound shuts itself in sleep,
As water closes round the oar,
And as no oar can wound the sea.
Confused, the senses waken
To a renewed delight,
She to herself has taken
Sea-music and sea-light.

ALLEGRE

Some mornings are as full of elation
As these pigeons crossing the hill slopes,
Silver as they veer in sunlight and white
On the warm blue shadows of the range.

And the sunward sides of the shacks
Gilded, as though this was Italy.

The bird's claws fasten round the lignum-vitae,
The roots of delight growing downward,
As the singer in his prime.

And the slopes of the forest this sunrise
Are thick with blue haze, as the colour
Of the woodsmoke from the first workman's fire.
A morning for wild bees and briersmoke,
For hands cupped to boys' mouths, the holloa
Of their cries in the cup of the valley.

The stream keeps its edges, wind-honed,
As the intellect is clear in affections,
Calm, with the rivulet's diligence.

Men are sawing with the wind on those ridges,
Trees arching, campeche, gommiers, canoe-wood,
The sawn trunks trundled down hillsides
To crash to the edge of the sea.
No temples, yet the fruits of intelligence,
No roots, yet the flowers of identity,
No cities, but white seas in sunlight,
Laughter and doves, like young Italy.

Yet to find the true self is still arduous,
And for us, especially, the elation can be useless and empty
As this pale, blue ewer of the sky,
Loveliest in drought.

ROOTS

Merely a naturalist's notebook?
Then till our Homer with truer perception erect it,
Stripped of all memory of rhetoric,
As the peeled bark shows white;
Not, as when the blue mist unravelled Sorcière,
The mountain, our guests whispered, 'Switzerland.'
When they conquer you, you have to read their books,
Then violently, false folklorique follows;
Maidenheads, or otherwise, arrowheads,
Their two archaeological pursuits.

May this make without pomp, without stone acanthus,
In our time, in the time of this phrase, a 'flowering of islands',
The hard coral light which breaks on the coast, near
Vieuxfort, as lucent as verse should be written;
Make the rice fields and guinea-corn waving,
The creak of the bullock-cart, make
The fields with bent Indians in the rice marsh.

All else will go down, the ambitions, divisions go down,
And love will go down, how long since Lesbia rotted?
Lesbia has rotted, and with Lesbia, Valerius Catullus,
                               Lesbia's saddle.
'And Troy upon this basis has been down,'
And Helen, old Helen lying alone in bed
These thousand years.
And yet remains, ruins for one 'cameo'
Ocelle insularum, our Sirmio.

That was Vigie, and when
The sea still beats against the ageing wall,
And the stone turrets filled with shaken leaves
When the wind brings the harbour rain in sheaves,
The yellow fort looks from the historic hill,
(As it were Poussin, or fragment from Bellini)

Its racial quarrels blown like smoke to sea
From all that sorrow, beauty is our gain,
Though it may not seem so
To an old fisherman rowing home in the rain.

PAYS NATAL

Your gaze, so full of sadness,
Contained the emptiness of long canoes,
The patience of brown rivers,
In those eyes was the sorrow of villages.
The touch of your fingers was sand
Brittle and hot in the forenoon,
Your forehead was an unmarked beach
Where no shadowy thoughts pass.

Like the scent of fresh-cut grass
Was the hair at the nape of your neck,
Sweat-pearled, each drop a goblet,
And your breath, as in sea-conch forever,
Was the ancient sigh of the sea.
Your teeth were white pebbles on an unknown beach,
In your speech
Was the clearness of the curled wave,
Green crystal in dead of noon,
In it was neither cunning nor subtlety.

In your flesh was the cool darkness
Of the first night wind on the beach,
Or as in drought, the first rains.
Your pride was imperial as sea-palms,
Where your feet rest is my country.
I might...
I might have gathered those senses in my arms,
As weary fishermen their honest seines.

EN MI-CARÊME

Should I compare that lady to this landscape
Being one with it when she is not within it,
Tradition would find in her the grace of trees,
Old ears hear flutes and the crisp lurch of foam
When in blue silence it is only the flowers
Falling, and dry palmettos their sea-noise in the breeze
To such spare music has this country come.

Suppose I, who saw her lately, caught in her speech,
Soothed as in drought, by the imagined sea,
The conch's immortal longing for that beach
She caught her first and only music on,
Or in a gentle heave of recollection,
Heard in her voice, leaves on a coral road,
A road empty and sighing in the sun?

A sea of cobalt harshness, without cloud,
Or let a cloud pass, and it makes
Of that sea-change, merry viridian,
Such simple metamorphoses she takes,
Both natures in their naturalness are one.

Or as the dry earth has its secret place,
Sweetest being so secret, during drouth,
Nature has filled her with an earthly grace
As clear as water in a clay carafe.
I see that lady and have heard her laugh.
I am parched with absence. My mouth burns for that mouth.

A SEA-CHANTEY

Là, tout n'est qu'ordre et beauté,
Luxe, calme, et volupté.

    Anguilla, Adina,
    Antigua, Cannelles,
    Andreuille, all the l's,
    Voyelles, of the liquid Antilles,
    The names tremble like needles
    Of anchored frigates,
    Yachts tranquil as lilies,
    In ports of calm coral,
    The lithe, ebony hulls
    Of strait-stitching schooners,
    The needles of their masts
    That thread archipelagoes
    Refracted embroidery
    In feverish waters
    Of the sea-farer's islands,
    Their shorn, leaning palms,
    Shaft of Odysseus,
    Cyclopic volcanoes,
    Creak their own histories,
    In the peace of green anchorage;
    Flight, and Phyllis,
    Returned from the Grenadines,
    Names entered this sabbath,
    In the port-clerk's register;
    Their baptismal names,
    The sea's liquid letters,
    Repos donnez a cils...
    And their blazing cargoes
    Of charcoal and oranges;
    Quiet, the fury of their ropes.

Daybreak is breaking
On the green chrome water,
The white herons of yachts
Are at sabbath communion,
The histories of schooners
Are murmured in coral,
Their cargoes of sponges
On sandspits of islets
Barques white as white salt
Of acrid Saint Maarten,
Hulls crusted with barnacles,
Holds foul with great turtles,
Whose ship-boys have seen
The blue heave of Leviathan,
A sea-faring, Christian,
And intrepid people.

Now an apprentice washes his cheeks
With salt water and sunlight.

In the middle of the harbour
A fish breaks the Sabbath
With a silvery leap.
The scales fall from him
In a tinkle of church-bells;
The town streets are orange
With the week-ripened sunlight,
Balanced on the bowsprit
A young sailor is playing
His grandfather's chantey
On a trembling mouth-organ.
The music curls, dwindling
Like smoke from blue galleys,
To dissolve near the mountains.

The music uncurls with
The soft vowels of inlets,
The christening of vessels,
The titles of portages,
The colours of sea-grapes,
The tartness of sea-almonds,
The alphabet of church-bells,
The peace of white horses,
The pastures of ports,
The litany of islands,
The rosary of archipelagoes,
Anguilla, Antigua,
Virgin of Guadeloupe,
And stone-white Grenada
Of sunlight and pigeons,
The amen of calm waters,
The amen of calm waters,
The amen of calm waters.

CONQUEROR

'March of Triumph'

This bronze, praised flayer of horses, who bred
Direction not valour in armies, has halted
On the crest of a ridge, in drizzling light;
His scaled gloves at rest
On the pommels, the wet-metal blaze
Of the sun in his sunken eye,
At the still, directionless hour
Of a changing, dragonish sky.

Iron deliverer whom the furies choose!
Half-human and half-deity in repose,
Envying each victim as its ravening grows,
Aye, the invincible! but whose
Armour cages a sigh no slaughter can depose.

Below him a thin harvest rusts in rain,
Lean flocks come limping to the herder's fife.
In that brown light, a mounted traveller
Splashes a silver river scarcely flowing
Through banks of ageing poplars;
On those unconquered peaks, it may be snowing.
On amber landscapes, hardly true to life
Is laid sometimes the quiet of unknowing
That elsewhere murderous teeth champ and devour,
As if such art placated nature's laws.
The small furred beast, spent beyond trembling
Contains such peace between its torturer's claws.

Take these small sparrows, witless if you will
That in the frightful glory of this hour
Flirt with that armed mass quiet on the hill,
Who dip, twitter, alight
On windless pennons, on these iron sheaves;

What are they? Fables of innocence trusting in power,
Or natural thoughts that haunt their sources still?
If one cried out pity might shake the mind
Like a limp pennon in a sudden wind,
And joy remembered make rage the more.
And at that cry, the god must raise his hand
However wearily, and all respite end
In noise and neighing thunder, in a wealth
Of sounding brass and the conqueror, sighing descend
Down to the desolation of self.

THE HURRICANE

after Hokusai

Come where on this last shore of broken teeth
All spume and fury of snorting battle-horses,
Wild waves and trees are lashing their drenched hair
Like treacherous women come to grief,
In grey, uproarious war, charge after charge
Of hurtling cavalry shuddering the shore,
Deafening the birdless marge!
Find the storm's swirling core, and understand
That mad, old fisherman dancing on his barge,
Yelling and poling as it wheels around
Its hollow boasts of cataclysmic sound.

Study the grey storm streak his hair, and prize
More than those hoarse cauldrons heaven has upended
The salt delight of wrinkled eyes,
And his strange sorrow when all storms are ended.

THE POLISH RIDER

The grey horse, Death, in profile bears the young Titus
To dark woods by the dying coal of day;
The father, with worn vision portrays the son
Like Dürer's knight astride a Rozinante;
The horse disturbs more than the youth delights us.
The warrior turns his sure gaze for a second,
Assurance looks its father in the eye,
The inherited, bony hack heads accurately
Towards the symbolical forests that have beckoned
Such knights, squired by the scyther, where to lie.
But skill dispassionately praises the rider,
Despair details the grey, cadaverous steed,
The immortal image holds its murderer
In a clear gaze for the next age to read.

THE BANYAN TREE, OLD YEAR'S NIGHT

> Ah! que le monde est grand à la clarté des lampes!
> Aux yeux de souvenir que le monde est petit!
> BAUDELAIRE: 'Le Voyage'

I

In the damp park, no larger than a stamp,
The rainbow bulbs of the year's end are looped
To link the withered fountain, and each lamp
Flickers like echoes where small savages whooped.

The square was this town's centre, but its spokes
Burn like a petered pinwheel of dead streets,
Turning in mind the squibs of boyish jokes,
Candy-striped innocents and sticky sweets

Fading in lemon light, as ribbons fade;
Bring back the pumping major and the snails
Of tubas marching as the brass band played
For children punished in their window gaols,

And gusts of tumbling papers, babies, kites
Blown round the kiosk bandrails in the wind;
But now these ghosts like wan bulbs show the whites
Of vanished eyes, and absence crowds the mind.

Soaring from littered roots, blackened with rain,
With inaccessible arms the banyan tree
Heaves in the year's last drizzle to explain
What age could not, responsibility.

II

At this town's rotting edges foul canals
Race with assurance when bad weather pours
White rain and wind by which the paper sails
Of crouched, black children steer for little tours

Till the silt clogs them on the further bank;
And the barques tilt, sunk in short voyages.
Yet, as they dare each season, so I thank
What wind compelled my flight, whatever rages

Urged my impossible exile; so with this park
I study now, as exiles stamps from home,
Fearing those bulbs will hiss out in the dark,
The mind be swept of truths as by a broom.

Even on silvery days, that classic fount
Being withered to the root, its throat as hoarse
As the last nurse's cry, could not surmount
My growing fear with clarity from a source

No parent knew. Or did we march
To the brass tunes of truth? Did I divine
Some secret in the fountain's failing arch,
And was that infant melancholy mine?

If it were so, it still remains, its sources
Blank as the rain on the deserted mind,
Dumb as the ancient Indian tree that forces
Its grieving arms to keep the homeless wind.

IN A GREEN NIGHT

The orange tree, in various light,
Proclaims perfected fables now
That her last season's summer height
Bends from each over-burdened bough.

She has her winters and her spring,
Her moult of leaves, which in their fall
Reveal, as with each living thing,
Zones truer than the tropical.

For if by night each golden sun
Burns in a comfortable creed,
By noon harsh fires have begun
To quail those splendours which they feed.

Or mixtures of the dew and dust
That early shone her orbs of brass,
Mottle her splendours with the rust
She sought all summer to surpass.

By such strange, cyclic chemistry
That dooms and glories her at once
As green yet ageing orange tree,
The mind enspheres all circumstance.

No Florida loud with citron leaves
With crystal falls to heal this age
Shall calm the darkening fear that grieves
The loss of visionary rage.

Or if Time's fires seem to blight
The nature ripening into art,
Not the fierce noon or lampless night
Can quail the comprehending heart.

The orange tree, in various light
Proclaims that fable perfect now
That her last season's summer height
Bends from each over-burdened bough.

SIMPLY PASSING THROUGH

Travelling through counties framed in glass,
And as in any gallery, homeless, we
Yearn for such true lands of unlikeliness,
Their ageless children running through the grass,
Their lovers voiceless by a voiceless sea.

Time, hurtling on, holds nature in a glaze,
Fleeting, yet so proportionately caught
That every frame outdistances its thought;
Girlhood in early leaf, a freckled stream,
Until my image melting in its gaze
Faces the future like a troubled dream.
That field of flowers surging to a wood,
Those farms unravelling as on a reel,
Why feel that had we found them earlier some good
Could come out of a country change? We would
Have spoiled such places too. We would, we would...

CADAVER

'...a God kissing carrion'

The carcass focused in the traffic headlamps,
Poor old dogsbody, hybrid leonine,
In fact as gutless as a paper bag
Seemed, skirting it, contemptuously supine.

As if the mashed beast slept, with tail tucked under
Apparently in comfort more than fear;
Yet the prim silence, more sedate than sleep,
Volleyed each passerby in unheard thunder,
Though no samaritan doffed the conscious hat.

By the next bend dogsbody was forgotten;
Half-dead with sleep, the personal repose
Weighed living eyelids down, kept the kids quiet,
Their questions drying on a sticky breath.

But not for old dogsbody, round whose nose
Wise flies in metaphysical debate raised riot;
Some hissed that old dogsbody could feign sleeping,
Some flouted wolfish fangs to risk a proof;
Fruitless debate. Buzz, buzz was never enough
For any beast nor for its master's weeping.

ISLANDS

(for Margaret)

Merely to name them is the prose
Of diarists, to make you a name
For readers who like travellers praise
Their beds and beaches as the same;
But islands can only exist
If we have loved in them. I seek
As climate seeks its style, to write
Verse crisp as sand, clear as sunlight,
Cold as the curled wave, ordinary
As a tumbler of island water;
Yet, like a diarist, thereafter
I savour their salt-haunted rooms,
(Your body stirring the creased sea
Of crumpled sheets), whose mirrors lose
Our huddled, sleeping images,
Like words which love had hoped to use
Erased with the surf's pages.

So, like a diarist in sand,
I mark the peace with which you graced
Particular islands, descending
A narrow stair to light the lamps
Against the night surf's noises, shielding
A leaping mantle with one hand,
Or simply scaling fish for supper,
Onions, jack-fish, bread, red snapper;
And on each kiss the harsh sea-taste,
And how by moonlight you were made
To study most the surf's unyielding
Patience though it seems a waste.

BRONZE

Hammered to the serenity of copper,
Her drowsing mask with slitted eyes,
Cupped in a palm and quiet as a plaque,
By tears unrunnelled, guiltless of surprise,
Bathes in dawn's wind, the wild night hair blown back.

Those mottled marbles I admired,
Bone-coloured in their pagan calm,
Sea-flowering Aphrodite borne on shells,
That blunt, androgynous Venus with one arm,
Male-thighed Dianas in their hunting dells,
And Ledas lost in blizzards of the swan,
Not one of those in such fierce sex was fired
Or holds its cunning secret as this one
Of lasting bronze, art of a savage race,
Marble, bronze, ebonwood, white, creole, black.

The elongated eyes look Arawak,
Arawak or Carib, but nakedness unsurprised
By armoured men dividing jungle leaves,
The sun ablaze on helmet, breastplate, greaves;
They close in groaning irony at their rape,
For that earth-coloured flesh buries all men
In immolations mocked by the wild ape,
At that brute cry all civilizations crack.

The high-boned ridges of the drowsing cheek
Are Amerindian by West African,
And is there any Egypt in that head?

Though, by the books, it seems impossible;
Still, those flinched nostrils have smelt the dead
And in my book that's sibylline; our sibyl
Has seen worse death in our Egyptian past
Than ritualistic slaughter to a faith;

That metal peace was hammered in a blast
Of burning heaps of pyramidical dead. Those veins
Are coloured rivers of the violent slain,
Cooled by dawn's wind, like sea-wind over canes
Which the East Indian heaps with burning back.

The hair is night, its skeins are the night's winds,
Out of such savage, tangled roots was born
This monolithic, unforgiving face
Wrought in a furious kiln, in which each race
Expects its hundredth dawn.

p. 33